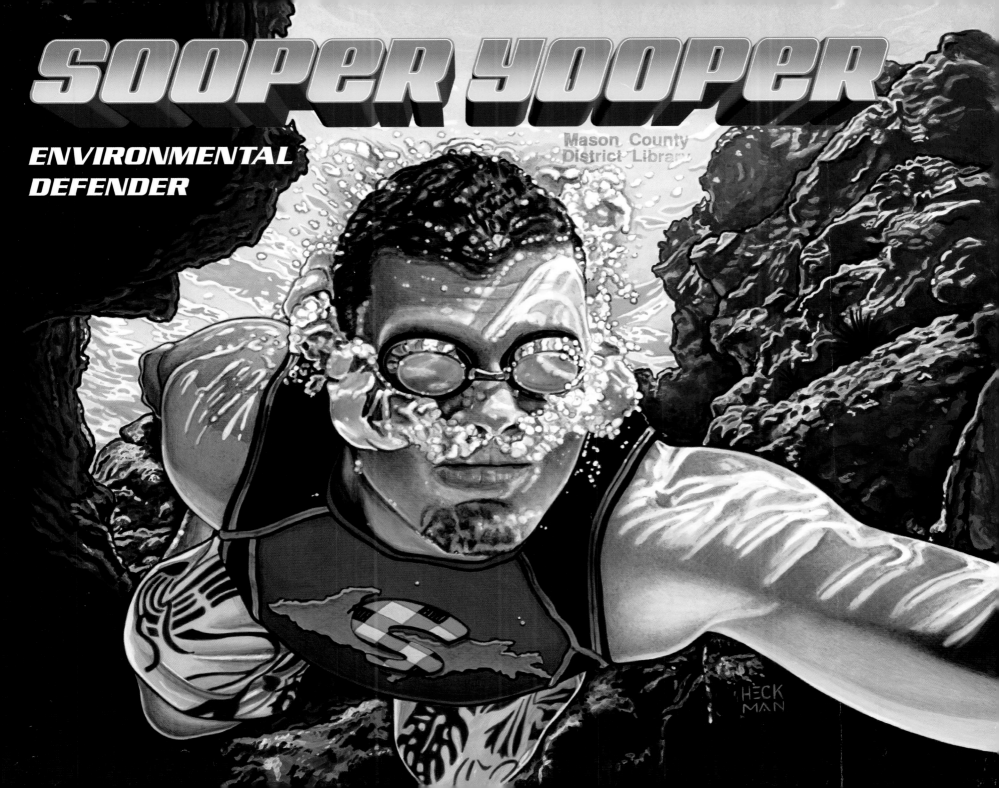

Undaunted Hero from the North
Battles Alien Sea Creatures

Published jointly by
The Wege Foundation, Grand Rapids, Michigan
and
Thunder Bay Press, Holt, Michigan

The Wege Foundation is honored to support Mark Heckman's "Sooper Yooper"
because Peter Wege believes the problem of exotic invasive species is the single biggest
threat to the Great Lakes. Mark Heckman's remarkable talent and his own love for the
Great Lakes makes this book vitally important to the young people who are our future.

ISBN: 978-1-933272-26-9

15   14   13   12   11   10   1   2   3   4   5   6   7   8   9

First Edition

Printed by Worzalla
Stevens Point, WI USA
June 2010

SOOPER YOOPER

Undaunted Hero from the North Battles Alien Sea Creatures

Illustrations & Concept
by Mark Heckman

Text by Mark Newman

To Beverly,
My mom's long-distance friend
Mark Newman

They call it Superior, one of the Great Lakes. Things lately, however, were not-so-great. They weren't even good.

There was trouble, and not just in River City. Sadly, Michigan's ecosystem of lakes, rivers, and streams was being invaded. Not by Martians. Not by anything out of the Twilight Zone. No, this threat was real and it caught the attention of one Billy Cooper.

Ex-Navy SEAL Billy Cooper was a military hero who enjoyed the water, specifically, crystal clear water untainted by human activity. But clear water was getting harder to find.

Cooper was a Yooper, which happens to be slang for someone living in Michigan's Upper Peninsula, but Cooper was no ordinary Yooper. He was a man with a mission, operating from his base in a converted lighthouse on the shores of the largest freshwater lake in the world.

The water, unfortunately, was becoming less fresh, and Cooper was the area's beacon of hope.

Cooper, with his trusty dog Mighty Mac at his side, recognized something needed to be done. He knew the state's supply of drinking water could be threatened or worse, eventually shut down.

"Semper fi-do, we've got work to do," Cooper called out to Mighty Mac while running on the dunes on a sunny, summer afternoon. It was a day that most would describe as beautiful, but Cooper saw that there could be dark clouds ahead.

Cooper saw the signs of trouble. The tide of tainted trout told him something was fishy, and he was certain that the number of dead loons and gulls dotting the beaches was for the birds.

There was a time when a single creature could horrify a Black Lagoon; now the Great Lakes faced a problem 180 times worse. Invasive species of all kinds, including snake-like sea lamprey, were threatening the lakes' very existence.

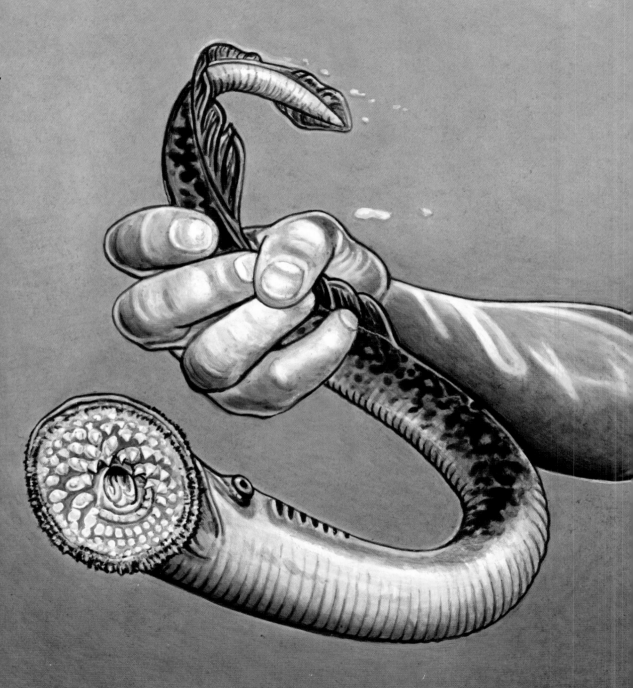

California has its Muscle Beach, but Cooper had no intention of letting his home state turn into Mussel Beach.

"Holy zooplankton!" cried Cooper, spotting more proof of an invasion.

Mighty Mac barked wildly from the shore. Sniffing out more menacing mollusks, he was doggone determined not to allow the problem to be buried.

Cooper collected water samples and took them to Grace, who worked in the lab at Lake Superior State University. He didn't need a rocket scientist to tell him there was something wrong with the water, but he hoped his chemist friend could pinpoint the source of trouble.

"Russian," Grace declared.

"I agree," Cooper replied, "we have to hurry if we're going to save the Great Lakes."

Grace eyed him suspiciously. She never was sure whether he was pulling her leg or not. "I'm talking about the discharge from a Russian freighter. Zebra mussels. Sea lampreys. Bug-eyed shrimp. These are not native to the Great Lakes. They come from all over the world when they're transported here in the ballasts of international ocean-going ships and then dumped into our freshwater."

From the Soo Locks to the Straits of Mackinac and all points beyond, every Great Lake was experiencing the same threat. You didn't need X-ray vision to see the problem.

Cooper and Mighty Mac had their hands full. They continued collecting fish and sending more samples to Grace. In the lab, she was able to analyze the genetic code of the invaders and isolate their DNA.

It didn't take long before they had their evidence. Grace was able to identify which nasty creatures were killing the native fish and birds. She was even able to narrow down the origin of the invasive species to a specific tributary of the Black Sea.

It was time for a trip to The Wedge.

Being an environmental defender was not without its costs. Cooper was fortunate to have the support of a green-minded philanthropist known as The Wedge.

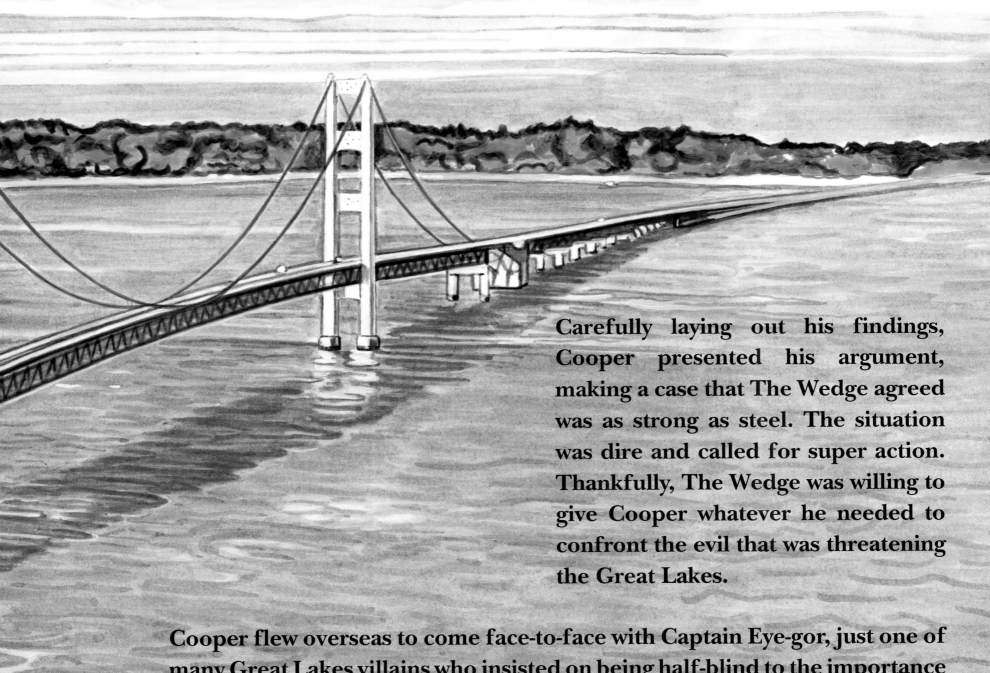

Carefully laying out his findings, Cooper presented his argument, making a case that The Wedge agreed was as strong as steel. The situation was dire and called for super action. Thankfully, The Wedge was willing to give Cooper whatever he needed to confront the evil that was threatening the Great Lakes.

Cooper flew overseas to come face-to-face with Captain Eye-gor, just one of many Great Lakes villains who insisted on being half-blind to the importance of protecting the environment.

"Stop spilling foreign species in our lakes," Cooper demanded.
"Put a cork in it. Or I will!"

"Did you come here to waste my time?" Captain Eye-gor complained.
"Why should I worry about such little fish? I have bigger fish to fry."

On his way back home, Cooper paid a visit to Congress. He laid down the law, or at least the way he saw things. He looked them in the eye. He told them that the future would be eerie if something wasn't done to stop the ocean-going "rust buckets" that were invading the Great Lakes from all over the world. Cooper was super persuasive.

The elected officials promised to act.

Cooper wasn't a politician but as an ex-Navy SEAL he knew how to fight battles. Whether flying in his whirlybird or cruising in his waterbug, Cooper got people's attention.

The U.S. Department of Transportation passed new regulations requiring all ocean-going vessels to flush out their ballast tanks with saltwater 200 nautical miles from any freshwater shore.

The politicians knew that if Cooper spotted more trouble,
he would act quickly.

Once back in Yooperland, Cooper continued his tireless efforts. With The Wedge's help, he would use every ounce of his being to stop any further invasions.

Armed with the new legislation, Cooper remained vigilant, as did the U.S. Coast Guard. The laws were a step in the right direction, but he knew that he and his loyal sidekick Mighty Mac would have to sniff out new dangers, like the issue of water diversion.

Protecting the Great Lakes, it seemed, didn't stop with foreign invaders. There were a number of western states looking into the idea of "borrowing" a little fresh water from their midwestern neighbors.

Billy Cooper, as always, was ready to take a stand. In fact, he had a little bit of advice, which he was only too happy to share.

"Back off suckers," Cooper proclaimed. "Water diversion is not going to happen here."

With the sun setting on another challenge, Billy Cooper, the Environmental Defender, was ready to recharge his batteries for the next battle.

SOOPER GLOSSARY

Ballasts: Tank-like compartments within a boat or ship that hold water. Ships carrying large cargo use ballast water for proper stability.

Black Lagoon: A reference to the old 3-D monster movie, Creature From the Black Lagoon.

Invasive Species: There are more than 180 fish, mussels, plants and other aquatic forms of life that don't belong in the Great Lakes.

Menacing Mollusks: Zebra mussels are small but prolific mollusks thought to have been carried from the Caspian Sea to the Great Lakes; they are menacing because they threaten city water supplies by clogging water-intake pipes.

Navy SEAL: An elite special force of the U.S. Navy known for dangerous missions. SEAL is short for Sea, Air and Land.

Philanthropist: A person who donates money, goods, services and/or time to support a cause.

Rust Buckets: Slang for aging ships that have seen better days.

Sea Lamprey: Snake-like creature that uses its teeth to penetrate the skin and scales of fish in its quest for blood.

Semper Fi-Do: Semper Fidelis, which is Latin for "Always Faithful," is often shortened to Semper Fi. Often associated with the U.S. Marines, the reference plays off a common nickname for dogs (Fido).

Soo Locks: Site that allows ships to travel between Lake Superior and the lower Great Lakes.

Tributary: A stream or river that flows into a primary body of water.

Water Diversion: The concept of taking water resources from the Great Lakes to other locations, with potentially negative impact on the region.

Yooper: A resident of Michigan's Upper Peninsula.

Zooplankton: Tiny animals that eat the organisms known as plankton and drift in the water columns of oceans and seas as well as bodies of fresh water.

Mark Heckman died in May 2010 after a two-year battle with non-Hodgkins lymphoma. He was an ardent advocate for environmental issues, and reaching young readers with a pro-earth message was extremely important to him.